W9-CES-932

21st Century Skills INNOVATION *Library*

From Gecko Feet to ...
Adhesive Tape

by Wil Mara

Published in the United States of America by Cherry Lake Publishing
Ann Arbor, Michigan
www.cherrylakepublishing.com

Content Adviser: Marjan Eggermont, Senior Instructor, Schulich School of Engineering, Calgary, Alberta, Canada

Reading Adviser: Marla Conn, ReadAbility, Inc.

Design: The Design Lab

Photo Credits: Cover background, page 3 background, and page 19, Image courtesy of Duncan Irschick and Alfred Crosby at the University of Massachusetts Amherst; cover left, Image courtesy of Duncan Irschick at the University of Massachusetts Amherst; cover right and page 3, Image courtesy of Michael Bartlett and Dan King, Crosby Research Group, University of Massachusetts Amherst; page 4, ©Erkki Alvenmod/Shutterstock.com; page 6, ©gresei/Shutterstock, Inc.; page 7, ©Sinisa Botas/Shutterstock, Inc.; page 9, ©infografick/Shutterstock, Inc.; page 10, ©Cathy Keifer/Shutterstock, Inc.; page 13, ©DDCoral/Shutterstock, Inc.; page 14, ©AlessandroZocc/Shutterstock, Inc.; page 15, Image courtesy of Michael Bartlett and Dan King, Crosby Research Group, University of Massachusetts Amherst; page 17, ©Georgios Kollidas/Dreamstime.com; page 19, Image courtesy of Duncan Irschick and Alfred Crosby at the University of Massachusetts Amherst; page 20, ©Blend Images/Shutterstock, Inc.; page 21, ©Aspen Photo/Shutterstock, Inc.; page 23, ©Greg Epperson/Shutterstock, Inc.; page 25, ©Natali Glado/Shutterstock, Inc.; page 27, ©AP photo/Scanpix Sweden/Henrik Montgomery.

Library of Congress Cataloging-in-Publication Data
Mara, Wil.
 From gecko feet to adhesive tape / by Wil Mara.
   pages cm.–(Innovations From Nature)
 Includes bibliographical references and index.
 ISBN 978-1-62431-752-1 (lib. bdg.) – ISBN 978-1-62431-764-4 (pdf) –
ISBN 978-1-62431-758-3 (pbk.) –ISBN 978-1-62431-770-5 (e-book)
 1. Adhesives–Juvenile literature. 2. Adhesive tape–Juvenile literature. 3. Geckos–Anatomy–Juvenile literature.
4. Biomimicry–Juvenile literature. 5. Inventions–Juvenile literature. I. Title.
TP968.M28 2014
668'.3–dc23   2013030375

Cherry Lake Publishing would like to acknowledge the work of
The Partnership for 21st Century Skills.
Please visit www.p21.org for more information.

Printed in the United States of America
Corporate Graphics Inc.
January 2014

CONTENTS

INNOVATIONS FROM NATURE

CHAPTER ONE

A Sticky Situation

Have you ever wondered how a fly can stick to almost any surface?

Imagine you are sitting on the couch, watching your favorite TV show. Suddenly, a fly zooms past your face. It heads for the ceiling, turns itself upside down, and sticks there. You lose interest in the TV as you watch this amazing animal crawl across your ceiling. You wonder what it would be like to stick to surfaces like the fly can. You're just a human being, though.

You can't climb up walls or hang from ceilings.
Or can you?

An **adhesive** is a substance that enables one thing to stick to another. The sticky stuff on a piece of tape is an adhesive. So is the stuff that keeps a Band-Aid on your skin. Glue and paste are adhesives. So are cement and beeswax.

Humans have been using adhesives for thousands of years. The earliest known man-made adhesive was made from tar. It was used to hold two stones together. Evidence of this ancient adhesive was discovered in Italy in 2001. It is believed to be more than 200,000 years old. Sticky substances for repairing pottery were first used around 4000 BCE. Simple cements for making art and decorations were used thousands of years ago in ancient Babylonia.

Glue plants were grown in Holland in the late 1600s. In 1750, England issued the first **patent** for glue. The glue was made from dead fish. It may sound gross, but it worked. Glues and other adhesives were widely used in America by the early 1800s. In 1848, an inventor named Henry Day patented early forms of tape in the United States. Other adhesives, such as the pressure-sensitive tape we use today, were developed in the early 1900s.

Today, adhesives are classified into two basic kinds—reactive and nonreactive. Reactive adhesives are not sticky on their own. Something needs to happen to them before they will work. A good example of this is simple modeling glue. The glue is a liquid when it is in a bottle. When you spread the glue onto something, the air in the room begins causing the glue to dry out. As the glue dries, it forms a bond with the objects it is touching. While the glue is still wet, you can easily pull apart the things it is stuck to. Once it is dry, it becomes very strong.

Nonreactive adhesives are always sticky. One example would be the sticky side of a piece of tape. As soon as the

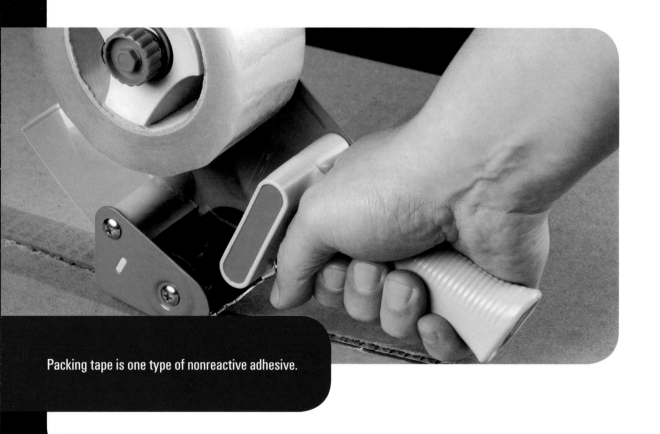

Packing tape is one type of nonreactive adhesive.

tape touches something, it forms a bond. It is difficult to pull the tape off something once you stick it on.

One thing about adhesives that has frustrated people for ages is that they are difficult to remove when they are no longer needed. For example, if you try to remove tape from a piece of paper, the paper usually rips. If you peel a price sticker off something you bought, it often leaves behind a layer of sticky adhesive. Wouldn't it be great if there were an adhesive that was incredibly strong and yet left no traces behind after you were done using it? What

21st Century Content

Scientists and engineers closely examine everything around them as they search for new ideas. Today, many of these inventors are looking to nature for inspiration. This is known as **biomimicry**. Biomimicry aims to create more **sustainable** products by imitating the abilities of plants or animals. Many inventors hope that products created using biomimicry will allow people to enjoy modern conveniences without harming the planet.

about an adhesive that could hold very heavy things together, even when used in a very small amount? Perhaps even something that you could use to climb up that wall in your living room and scale across the ceiling?

Such inventions might sound like science fiction, but not all of them are. Scientists and **engineers** have carefully observed the way lizards called geckos use their incredible feet to climb smooth surfaces and hang upside down. They have used their observations to create a new kind of adhesive. You might be crawling along the walls and ceiling of your living room sooner than you think!

CHAPTER TWO

The Missing Link

Geckos are lizards that can climb easily on almost any surface. Their feet have an adhesive quality that allows them to stick to everything from rocks to glass. This ability is so powerful that geckos can even hang upside down using just a single toe. These remarkable lizards have been around for a very long time. Experts have discovered gecko remains that are more than 100 million years old.

Like houseflies, geckos can stick to almost any surface.

However, the man-made technology that mimics the adhesive qualities of a gecko's feet is so new that most people don't even know about it yet.

The mystery of how geckos can adhere to just about any surface has puzzled researchers for ages. Some believed that geckos had tiny suction cups on their feet. Others believed that the gecko's feet produced a type of adhesive fluid. No one knew for sure. That changed in the 20th century.

The tokay gecko is one of the largest gecko species in the world.

In 1996, a team of scientists led by biologist Duncan Irschick was able to measure how just powerful a gecko's grip is. Their experiments included a variety of gecko and other lizard species. What they found was astounding. For example, they discovered that the two front feet of a tokay gecko could hold up to 4.5 pounds (2.0 kilograms) of force. The tokay is one of the largest geckos. Adult tokays can reach a length of 12 inches (30 centimeters) and weigh as much as 7 ounces (200 grams). Its smaller, lighter relatives were just as good at sticking to surfaces, too.

Scientists around the world started looking for ways to apply this to a product that people could use. They wanted to imitate a gecko's foot to create an easily removable and reusable adhesive. Some researchers, such as Kellar Autumn and biologist Andre Geim, focused on the gecko's **setae**. A gecko has millions these tiny hairs on each foot. Each setae branches off into thousands of even tinier pad-like objects called **spatulae**. Each spatula measures no more than two-billionths of a centimeter wide.

The spatulae make contact with a surface each time a gecko stops. When this happens, the **molecules** of the spatulae and the surface are drawn to each other. This means that each spatula forms a weak bond with the

Learning & Innovation Skills

In addition to the gecko's adhesive powers, scientists are interested in the way setae seem to be self-cleaning. After years of further study, they have determined that a gecko's rolling and unrolling walking motion forces dirt out from between the setae. This means that the gecko's feet are cleaned with each step it takes. If successfully duplicated, this would permit an adhesive to be used over and over. It is yet another example of how learning the fine details of nature leads us to innovative ideas and terrific new products.

surface. There are so many spatulae on a gecko's foot that the overall connection adds up to a bond that is very strong.

Many researchers successfully created small adhesives based on setae and spatulae. But these adhesives could only hold small loads. Also, the tiny setae-like hairs became damaged with use. Something had to change before the adhesive could work on a bigger scale.

A team of researchers led by engineer Al Crosby was doing its own experiments at the University of Massachusetts. Like other scientists, they wanted to create a reusable adhesive. Crosby had done research on gecko setae, but it did not produce the results he wanted. He and his team looked for other ideas.

Crosby started to look beyond the setae and spatulae. He studied the research of biologists who investigated the full gecko anatomy, including tendons. Tendons are tough, relatively flexible cords of tissue that connect muscles to bone. The research connected back to biologist Anthony Russell, who had studied how tendons affect a gecko's adhesiveness in the 1980s. From all of these lessons, including Duncan Irschick's initial force measurements, Crosby and his research group argued that there was more to a gecko than its setae. To fully understand a gecko's ability to climb surfaces, a researcher had to look at the whole foot.

Researchers took a close look at gecko feet to learn how they worked.

CHAPTER THREE

The Bigger Picture

Crosby and Irschick found success by taking a gecko's entire foot into account.

Al Crosby and his team created an adhesive strip that could carry huge loads. One piece about the size of an index card could hold up to 700 pounds (318 kg). How did they do it? Surprisingly, their invention did not use setae or spatulae at all. Instead, it uses a structure similar to the gecko's entire foot, particularly its tendons.

In most animals, tendons connect their bones to their

Geckskin is shown here holding up a large television

Life & Career Skills

Inventing new things from scratch is one of humanity's greatest abilities. It is also one of our biggest challenges. Even when a great idea comes along, it can take a long time to turn it into something that actually works. Thomas Edison was one of the greatest inventors in history. However, he failed hundreds of times before he made the first working lightbulb. He did not consider those nonworking bulbs to be true failures. Instead, he saw them as a normal part of the creative process. It was no different with the scientists working on gecko-like adhesives. It took researchers around the world more than a decade before anyone came up with a product that worked correctly. If you believe in an idea, don't give up!

muscles. The tendons do not extend any farther. Geckos have tendon-like structures in their feet that connect to the skin. The tendon is stiff and strong. But it is also thin, so it can bend. This makes a gecko's foot soft, so it can conform to a surface and create contact. The stiffness in the tendons holds this contact. To release, a gecko bends its toes back to break the contact.

This is what Crosby and his research group wanted to mimic in their adhesive. They needed something soft that could drape over a surface and create contact. But the object also had to be stiff in order to keep the contact and carry a high load. What they created was Geckskin.

Crosby and his Ph.D. student, Michael Bartlett, started with a stiff woven fabric. They added a soft, **synthetic** material called a

In addition to the lightbulb, Thomas Edison invented the movie camera, the record player, and countless other devices.

polymer. The fabric draped over an object and the soft polymer created contact. Then the stiff material held the contact. If a person tries to pull it along the surface, the adhesive wouldn't move. But the adhesive comes right off if the person pulls it up and away from a surface, just like a gecko's toe bending back.

Crosby and his team wanted to demonstrate how these the concepts of draping and stiffness apply to the adhesive performance of living geckos. They searched for the word "gecko" and their university online—and found out Duncan Irschick had recently joined the biology department of their own university! When they approached him, Irschick quickly agreed to work with Crosby and his team. Their studies led to some exciting results.

Geckskin is made up of a strong, woven fabric.

CHAPTER FOUR

Today and Tomorrow

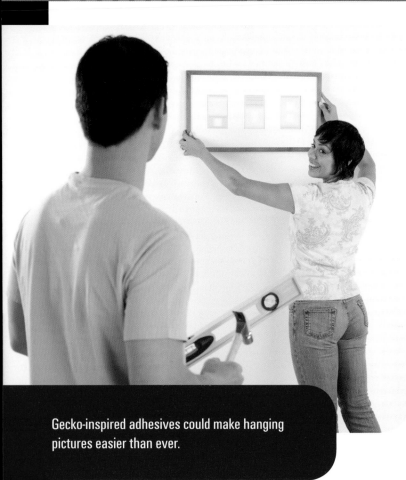

Gecko-inspired adhesives could make hanging pictures easier than ever.

Crosby, Irschick, and their team continue to improve Geckskin. The team hopes to have a product ready to be sold in stores soon.

They are not the only ones still working. A wide variety of researchers are looking into new ideas in a range of fields. One group is working on a bandage

Gecko gloves might one day make it easy for anyone to catch a football like a pro.

that may one day patch wounds inside the human body. Others are applying it to robots used by the military. The potential uses for gecko-inspired adhesive products

21st Century Content

Another step in the innovation of gecko-adhesive products may soon come from the study of another creature in the natural world—the mollusk. Mollusks are a group of sea creatures that include everything from tiny mussels to huge squids and octopuses. A mollusk's body produces substances that might be able to be copied synthetically and combined with gecko-inspired adhesives. Some researchers believe that this combination would produce a material that could stick to just about any surface in both dry and wet environments. Such material would have countless uses, including bandages that hold tight in water.

are nearly endless. People have found possible uses for them from sports and robotics, to medicine and home improvement. Imagine how easy it would be to hang a painting or a television. Driving nails or screws into walls would become a thing of the past. Strips of adhesive could be attached to the bottoms of sneakers and the palms of gloves, and people could scale walls and crawl across ceilings. Rock climbing would be made considerably safer. So would washing windows in tall buildings or repairing a roof. Militaries could also make use of this amazing technology. Soldiers would be able to scale any surface quickly and quietly.

The possibilities do not end there. Geckskin has affected more than technology. Biology has also changed. The research behind Geckskin answered some questions about geckos. But it asked many more. In fact, the Geckskin scientists

Rock climbers, who use ropes and clips to keep from falling, might one day be able to climb more easily using gecko tape.

were granted money to do more research not just on gecko adhesion, but also other animals. As their and other scientists' work continues, who knows what types of products will one day be available on the grocery store shelf?

CHAPTER FIVE

Minds at Work

Gecko-inspired adhesives are a very new idea. Because the technology holds such promise, there are already many people working to turn these dreams and visions into reality. Let's take a look at some of the most important figures in this growing field.

Anthony Russell was born and grew up in England, receiving his doctorate in zoology

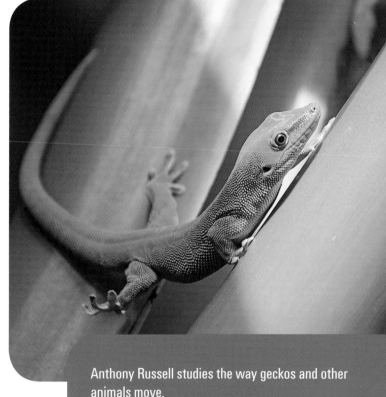

Anthony Russell studies the way geckos and other animals move.

Life & Career Skills

Engineering is a fascinating scientific field and one worth considering as a career choice. An engineer is a problem solver who uses his or her knowledge in many different areas—including aerospace, mining, computers, electronics, agriculture, architecture, and other fields. Engineers are required to exercise a high degree of creativity and innovative thinking. Engineers are often highly paid. If you choose a career in engineering, you'll most likely be challenged to push your talents to their limit, and you will have the chance to make the world a better place through your hard work.

at the University of London. Eventually, he made his way to the University of Calgary in Alberta, Canada, where he serves as an adjunct professor and performs research for the university and the Royal Tyrrell Museum of Paleontology. Much of his research focuses on how geckos developed their ability to adhere to surfaces. He published some of the foundational research on gecko feet and adhesion. He has also made breakthroughs in understanding how and when geckos gain traction in rugged terrain.

Andre Geim (1958–) was born in Russia and attended the Moscow Institute of Physics and Technology, where he received a doctorate in 1987. In 2001, he was appointed director of the Manchester Centre for Mesoscience and Nanotechnology. It was around this time that he

Dr. Andre Geim delivers a speech after winning the Nobel Prize in 2010.

and his fellow scientists began putting together the first samples of a workable gecko-inspired adhesive called gecko tape. Geim has also played a key role in

21st Century Content

There is little doubt that technologies based on biomimicry are going to play a big role in the future. The creation of synthetic setae is far from the only development in this area. There will be many more to come. New inventions that are environmentally friendly will be especially important as more people become aware of the need to keep our planet healthy. If you want to take part in these fascinating innovations and ride the wave of biomimicry, you should make a point of studying up on the natural sciences. Consider a career in a field where you can put your talents to good use. Such fields include engineering, biology, chemistry, design, environmental research, teaching, and medical professions.

developing a material known as graphene. Graphene is incredibly thin, but it is one of the strongest and hardest materials in the world. Geim's work with graphene earned him the 2010 Nobel Prize in Physics.

Kellar Autumn worked closely with Robert Full on the original breakthrough research of gecko adhesion. Today, he is a professor of biology at Lewis & Clark College in Portland, Oregon. He has continued his research into gecko adhesives and discovered that their setae are the only self-cleaning adhesives known in the natural world. He has also discovered that geckos use only about a third of the energy that other legged animals require in order to move about. As a result of his studies, Autumn has designed and patented the first "gecko glue," which may transform the adhesives industry worldwide.

Duncan Irschick was formerly a professor at Tulane University before joining the faculty at the University of Massachusetts Amherst. He is an expert in the field of animal movement, sometimes known as animal athletics. He has worked with species ranging from humans and rodents to reptiles and amphibians.

Alfred Crosby led the development of Geckskin. Crosby is a professor at the University of Massachusetts Amherst. He received his Ph.D. in Materials Science and Engineering from Northwestern University in 2000. He has studied many of the adhesive properties found in nature and tried to find ways to re-create them for use by humans. His Geckskin material was named one of 2012's top five scientific breakthroughs by CNN. Along with the gecko, he has also researched the incredible plant known as the Venus flytrap.

Glossary

adhesive (ad-HEE-siv) a substance, such as glue, that makes things stick together

biomimicry (bye-oh-MI-mi-kree) the practice of studying and copying nature's forms and systems to solve human problems

engineers (en-juh-NERZ) people who are specially trained to design and build things

molecules (MAH-luh-kyoolz) the smallest units that a substance can be divided into while still displaying all of its chemical properties

patent (PAT-uhnt) a legal document giving the inventor of an item the sole rights to manufacture or sell it

setae (SEE-tee) tiny hairlike structures found on the bottom of a gecko's foot

spatulae (SPA-cho-lie) microscopic pad-like objects, roughly broccoli-like in shape, found at the end of a gecko's setae

sustainable (suh-STAY-nuh-buhl) done in a way that can be continued and that doesn't use up natural resources

synthetic (sin-THET-ik) manufactured or artificial, rather than found in nature

For More Information

BOOKS

Connors, Kathleen. *Geckos*. New York: Gareth Stevens Publishing, 2013.

Gates, Phil. *Nature Got There First*. New York: Kingfisher, 2010.

Lee, Dora. *Biomimicry: Inventions Inspired by Nature*. Tonawanda, NY: Kids Can Press, 2011.

Marsico, Katie. *Geckos*. New York: Children's Press, 2013.

WEB SITES

Ask Nature: What Is Biomimicry?
www.asknature.org/article/view/what_is_biomimicry
Find out more about biomimicry with examples, links, and interesting video content.

Biomimicry 3.8
www.biomimicry.net
Check out the latest news on the science of biomimicry, with links to other sites as well as information about choosing a career in the field.

Index

About the Author

Wil Mara is the author of more than 140 books, many of which are educational titles for young readers. More information about his work can be found at www.wilmara.com.